the
Alphabet
of Balance

By
James G. Morrison

Designed by
Glen Eytchison

Forward
Bruno Mascolo, President & CEO TONI&GUY/TIGI

Published by The Three Letters, Inc.
14988 Sand Canyon, #8, Irvine, California 92618

Printing of this edition of The Alphabet of Balance
graciously sponsored by TONI&GUY/TIGI

The Alphabet of Balance

James G. Morrison

The Three Letters, Inc.
14988 Sand Canyon, #8, Irvine, California 92618

ISBN 0-9715755-0-9

Book Design: Glen Eytchison
Back Cover Photo: Danny Beruman
Production: Ben Dixon and Vincent Nguyen of Glen Eytchison Design; www.gedesign.com

Printed and bound in the United States.

Dedication

First of all to a loving mother for teaching me that all things are possible.

To a loving father for giving me a love of music, literature, a sense of fair play and a wicked sense of humor.

To a loving God who makes all things possible.

To Bruno—my business partner, my mentor, my friend.

To Charles, Catherine & John—I love you.

To Paul, Anthony, Pat and Guy—thank you for your friendship.

To Kay—thanks for all your help in the editing of the book, I love you.

To all my colleagues & the girls & guys in the rooms—you know who you are—thanks for the experience, strength & hope.

Special Thanks

To Kyara Mascolo and her crew.

To my very special friends—Bruce, Charlotte, Cam, Kenny, and Frank and Laurel Chirico—thank you very much for your support and friendship.

To Jon Broom, Wendy Hall, Thaddeus Jordan, Barbara Rush and Erika Stone of TONI&GUY/TIGI.

Forward

It is truly an honor for me to write a forward for my dear friend's first book.

Let me start by saying that I am very grateful to God for the friends He has sent to me. One of those friends that I'm so grateful for is James. James is not just a friend but a partner. A partner in business, and a life friend. I met him many years ago and I knew, throughout all those years, that James was an extremely talented person. But when I read his book, I realized his talent goes outside the limits of any industry, any field.

I am impressed by the capacity he has to list, in the most simple and beautiful way and from A to Z, the key thoughts we must never forget. The basic, but easy to take for granted "substance of life."

Several, if not all of the paragraphs, I read twice, thrice, sometimes more times. Most of them took me to another level, another atmosphere where I applied them to my own personal experience. Others reminded me of things long forgotten and still others have taught new elements that I am sure will give me the passport to develop my own blueprint, my own guide to acquire balance.

This book has given me "food for thought", it has given me the opportunity to visualize the four corners of balance, to stop and think which one is the one that I have to pay more attention to, is it the spiritual, the emotional, the mental? Or perhaps the physical?

The Alphabet of Balance has opened a new door for me. It has helped me to comprehend that in order to achieve success in life we must create our personal harmony.

From now on, every time that I find myself in a scenario where I could be set off of balance, I will say to myself: "Refer to The Alphabet of Balance."

Thank you James, for sharing with me your passion for life.

Bruno Mascolo, President & CEO TONI&GUY/TIGI

Introduction

The reason I was inspired to write this book was due to the interest shown by colleagues of mine in my industry who were participating in one of my motivational seminars with the focus on creating balance.

The Alphabet of Balance is a personal viewpoint as to my definition of success. In a word, my definition is Harmony – nothing more, nothing less. It is from my observations based upon my personal interaction with people in my life and my own experiences.

The book's ideas are based on different philosophies from different theologies, spiritual beliefs and cultures, and upon the success of my individual experiences in applying them in my everyday life.

My intent with this book is not to become a guru nor to promote a particular point of view, but to share my experience, strength and hope so that we all can stay in harmony with our inner gurus. I have chosen to use the alphabet layout that is almost like my seminar format.

I hope you will find it useful in your own personal journey and that it will assist you in achieving the balance you so deserve in your life.

acceptance

acknowledgement

action

ask

attitude

Acceptance

We accept where we are today in all areas of our lives. We know our relationship to family, friends, career, coworkers, and our own inner selves, is a direct result of the choices we've made. The accountability is squarely on our shoulders and empowers us because it is an awareness that absolves any second or third party of any blame or responsibility for our life situation.

Acknowledgement

We respond positively to acknowledgement for a job well done or congratulations for going the extra mile; thanking a family member, friend or coworker for his assistance. By taking the time to say thank you, we continually acknowledge each other, and this can be more rewarding than receiving material compensations.

Action

A journey of a thousand miles starts with the first step. We have often heard that the road to hell is "paved with good intentions". The difference between what we say and what we do is how the world sees us. Action is where the rubber meets the road. It's putting one foot in front of the other and taking the first step. Certainly the actions we take in our relationships, speak loudly of who we are.

Ask

We ask open-ended questions that require more than just yes and no answers. "Do you like living here?" changes to "tell me why you like living here." We continually seek knowledge.

Attitude

The attitude we carry with us can make or break us in attracting and maintaining healthy relationships. Our accomplishments are directly influenced by the attitudes we carry with us. We bring our attitude into play as a guideline in our evaluations of others and their actions - that person has a "winning" attitude, or that person has "attitude". Attitude separates the can do's from the cannot's. Success is born of the attitude of gratitude, and that generates abundance. We pull in all of life's gifts when we are grateful for and grateful to. Motto: "Grateful people are happy people, and those that aren't, aren't."

Balance

Be

Beauty

Beach

Believe

Brainstorm

Balance

The four corners of balance are spiritual, emotional, mental and physical. Attention to these promotes balance in each area of our lives: financial, social, creative, and business. Scheduling our priorities makes more sense than prioritizing our schedules, the difference being that we have the power to have whatever is important to us in our daily lives such as prayer and meditation, physical exercise, a fulfilling and lucrative career, family, friends, and creative outlets such as music and art. It is easy for us to see when immersion in one area sets us off balance in all of the other areas. The balance we bring to our life gives us personal boundaries and the right to fulfill our life's mission.

Be

To be where our hands are gives us the ability to be present in the here and now. It connects the body and the mind and makes our interaction fluid. When someone is communicating with us we are present and able to listen and respond appropriately. This is especially important to our relationships with our family, friends and coworkers—to offer them the undivided attention they deserve. We be: mindful and in the moment, gracious and open, our own best friend.

Beach

We cannot get wet standing on the shore…Refer to Action!

Beauty

There is beauty in every step.

Believe

In order to achieve, we have to believe – in our own personal balance, in the goodness of life, in our deserving the best life has to offer us. Believing that there are no mistakes and that we are indeed part of the cycle of life gives us faith that we have our place in the world and our role to fulfill. Belief fosters faith, faith enables us to have positive experiences, and those experiences give us knowledge to pass on to others for everyone's benefit.

Brainstorm

When we get bored, we let our imaginations run by using music, film, nature, silence and especially collaboration with our friends and family. Thus we come up with the most creative and original innovations. Refer to Action.

Care
Celebrate
Chance
Change
Choice
Civility
Control
Confidence
Contribution
Commitment

Care

People don't care about what we know until they know we care.

Celebrate

One of my friends had a sister who was diagnosed with terminal cancer and had lived a fairly isolated life without many friends or interests. Upon hearing about her sister's condition, my friend took a trip to London to visit her and take her to tour the museums and take in some shows. Her sister was actually not really concerned about dying, as she clearly had not been living a passionate life. During the trip, they had an amazing time, and my friend's comment about her ill sister was, "She was sad at the thought of dying, but so happy to finally be celebrating life. She realized just how much fun life could be."

Chance

We take some chances as not everything can be calculated ahead of time. Some decisions have to be based upon intuition or gut feelings. If we never were to take a chance, we certainly would not fail, but would probably not expand our potential. The reward for taking healthy chances is the realization of infinite possibilities.

Change

Significant in our development as humans is how we change and grow. Real change comes from the inside, and if we don't go within, we go without on many levels. We look over our fears, concerns, strengths and shortcomings so that we get to know who we truly are. This is the healthy approach to change. We learn to shift from the unhealthy pattern of trying to fill ourselves with things from this material world to the inner journey of self-revelation.

Choice

Success is a choice, not an accident. As successful people we take actions with accountability that unsuccessful people do not.

Civility

We find that civility costs nothing to give and there is no charge for receiving it.

Control

The only thing we can ever control is our actions, our words, and the perspective we are willing to entertain. We cannot control anyone or anything outside of ourselves. Attempting to do so can drive us to major distraction and can affect our relationships with others. Refer to Acceptance.

Confidence

We are confident that we do not need material things to make us feel complete. We educate ourselves thoroughly so that we become effective in our personal and business relationships. This develops confidence. How we develop comes from our understanding, our positive experiences, and what we are able to learn from all who are examples in our everyday surroundings: our mentors, our family, our friends, our coworkers and our educational resources.

Contribution

We want to be part of our working solution and to feel involved. We give feedback and support to each other in a positive way. We support that which we contribute to and it gives us a sense of ownership, pride and being a part of something bigger than ourselves.

Commitment

Showing up is how we keep our obligations. Eighty percent of our success is because showing up enables us to be where we say we will be, when we say we will be there and doing what we say we will do.

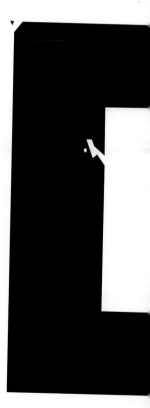

Definition

Difference between an amateur and a professional: when an amateur makes a mistake we say, "Oops", and when a professional makes a mistake we say, "That looks interesting."

Denial

When we see the world not as it is, but as we are pretending it to be.

Detachment

The more invested we are in the outcome of any action we take, the more it costs us when the outcome doesn't go as we planned. Detachment allows us to keep our inner core strong while letting go of all outside events and situations and thereby ensuring that our challenges do not rock our foundation. Whenever we are going through a difficult time in life, our emotions can cause us great pain, and while pain is mandatory, certainly, suffering is optional.

Discipline

Success without sacrifice is not success at all and is akin to receiving something that is handed to us without some degree of merit or effort on our part. Naturally we are going to benefit from the gifts we receive, but discipline in our life is an essential ingredient of successful balance.

Dreams

All of the buildings, bridges, inventions, books written and music composed were first born of dreams and dreamers. We dare to dream big.

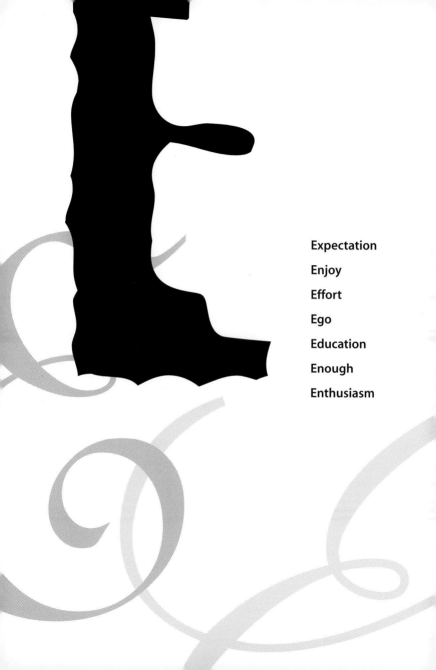

Expectation

Enjoy

Effort

Ego

Education

Enough

Enthusiasm

Education

Is about lifelong learning.

Effort

80% of our results come from 20% of our energy, and the more of our focus we channel to the task at hand, the more present we are and hence, the more successful our results. Refer to Be.

Ego

A little word that makes a huge impact. Ego can stand for many things: Earth Going Only, Either God Or, Empty Grasp On. We melt this iceberg when we leave it exposed, when we focus on yours and not mine, when we worry more about what we think of ourselves than what others think of us. When we do not make decisions out of ego and pride, we make them with love and clarity. When we turn the negative into positive we get to Embrace God & Orbit or Enhance, Grow & Overturn. Refer to Progress.

Enough

We can have enough – it is a choice we make in our favor.

Enthusiasm

Is contagious. When we are truly enthused we feel God's pleasure running through us.

Expectation

The more realistic our expectation, the less disappointment we will experience. Resentment comes when we don't get our expectations met, so we attempt to free ourselves from this whenever possible; we are willing to be open to whatever comes our way. We might as well - it's going to come regardless. Refer to Control.

Enjoy

We stop and smell the roses because our journey is a long-lasting marathon to be lived - not a mere sprint.

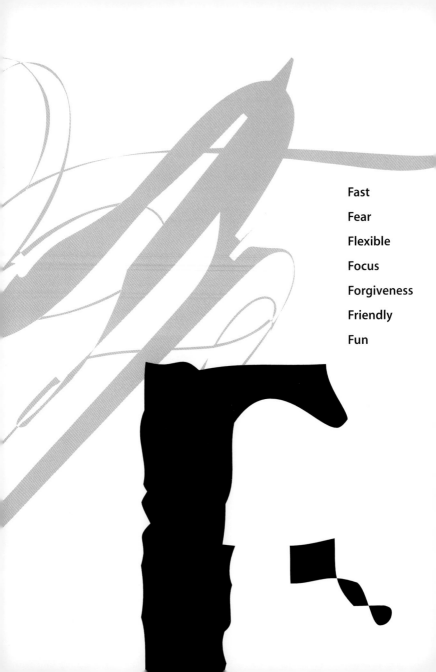

Fast

Fear

Flexible

Focus

Forgiveness

Friendly

Fun

Fast

We are efficient and our friends, family and coworkers are impressed by our quick, correct, and appropriate responses to their wishes.

Fear

We encounter different kinds of fear: healthy fear that protects us from harm, intuitive fear that tells us to use caution, and practical fear that we pull from our life experience. Our unhealthy fears breed self-doubt, low self-esteem, envy, anger and a multitude of other foes. We work to identify fear so that we can get to its source by using our spiritual tools: journaling, discussing them with a trusted friend, helping others, and the most important tool, faith. "No Fear" is probably not realistic, but to Know Fear is essential. Faith is the natural anecdote to fear. We continually take stock of our emotional state by asking, "What would I do if I weren't afraid?" and "What is the fear that prevents me from achieving my life goals?" Mark Twain said, "I have been through some really terrible things in my life and some of them have actually happened."

Flexible

There is always a little gray area!

Focus

We focus on the task at hand. We finish what we start.

Forgiveness

We can easily give in to anger when we feel wronged, or we can wish for revenge. We can swallow the poison of our anger and wish the other person would get ill from it, but the reality is, whatever we do to another we are in fact doing to ourselves. We ask ourselves these questions: Who is one person that I feel I need to forgive in my business life? Who is one person I need to forgive in my personal life? What qualities in myself do I need to forgive?

Friendly

People like to be with people they like. We work
at being the kind of friend we want to have!

Fun

We never forget to have fun! We enjoy
the journey and don't take it all so
seriously. We remember that one day
we will be fertilizer for the daisies.

Refer to Balance.

Give

Goals

God's Handiwork

Give

We give generously knowing that sharing is the way to keep what we have.

Goals

We begin with the end in mind. Dreams with deadlines are goals. We list the things we want to accomplish for the year. We measure our progress daily, weekly and monthly but remember to avoid going into overwhelm. We focus on our priorities. Refer to both Action and Chance.

God's Handiwork

When we look at trees, ocean, sky, stars, each blade of grass, and every person we meet, we realize there are no mistakes, just a perfect plan of which we are a part, and at that moment we claim our place in the world. We know that it doesn't need proving, justifying, mystifying – just accepting. Refer to Acceptance.

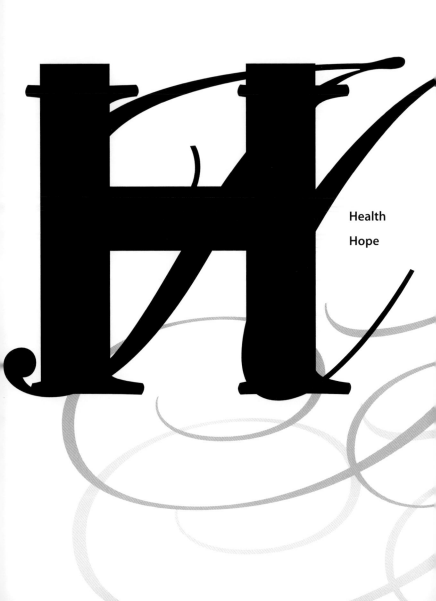

Health

Hope

Health

Striving for health and well being in each and every area of our lives is the foundation on which our lives are built. We bring this to our relationships.

Hope

Hope floats.

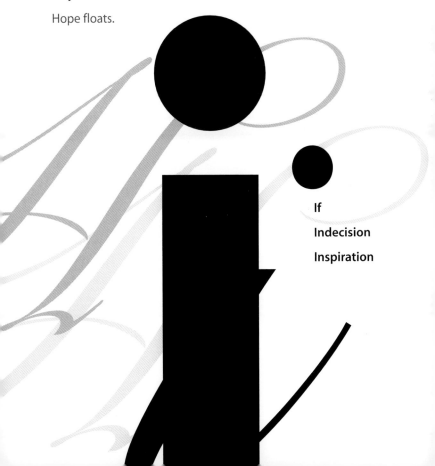

If

Indecision

Inspiration

If

If we practice old behavior patterns we get old results.

If we love someone we set him or her free and if they return we know it was meant to be.

If we are doing what we truly love to do, then we never work another day of our lives!

If we concentrate on being the best we can be, learning our profession, the financial rewards do come.

If we concentrate on making money, we may not be good at what we do and we may not get the joy and fulfillment that we are entitled to.

If we concentrate on the job at hand the end result far surpasses any possibilities we imagined.

Indecision

Occasionally we are reluctant to resolve a pending matter. As we consider all the facts and ramifications, we hesitate. We are aware of this state of consciousness and work continually to settle the matter and take purposeful, positive action.

Inspiration

Inspiration is the true power behind us as we create harmony in our life. It is that feeling inside us that resonates and urges us to expand to the depth of our life force. We get inspiration from art, architecture, music, friends and family, and as a result of participating. Inspiration truly is "in the spirit."

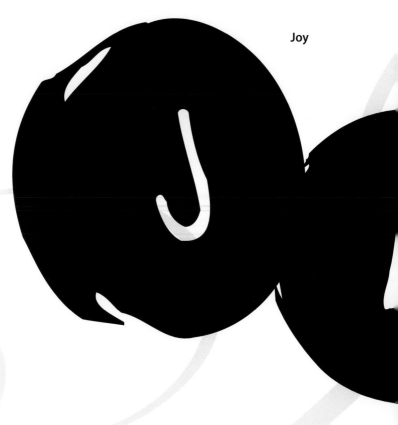

Joy

We discover the joy in each moment, in each day, and in each person we meet.

Knowing

We know this: Just because we think it, doesn't make it so!

We know what we want but mostly get what we need.

Knowing

Listen

We learn and then do better at what we already know.

We lead by example.

We laugh at ourselves.

We remember our motto: Life is good, people are fantastic, and business is great.

Listen

We listen without prejudice. We have two ears and one mouth and practice listening twice as much as we speak.

Mirror

Mission

Message

Mentor

Move

Mirror

Life mirrors to us exactly what we need so that our most painful moments become our greatest lessons, and the most difficult people around us become our greatest teachers.

Mission

Our personal toolbox contains a mission statement that is helpful in keeping us true to our goals. Our statement is concise, precise, passionate, motivational and realistic. It has the power to move us emotionally, spiritually and physically.

Message

Our lives broadcast our message to the world, and we work to live our message.

Mentor

We see further because we are willing to stand on the shoulders of the giants around us. We mentor each other.

Move

We cannot go into the future looking in our rear view mirrors.

Nurture

We nurture ourselves, our talents, each other.

Options

We see that our options are more useful than our excuses.

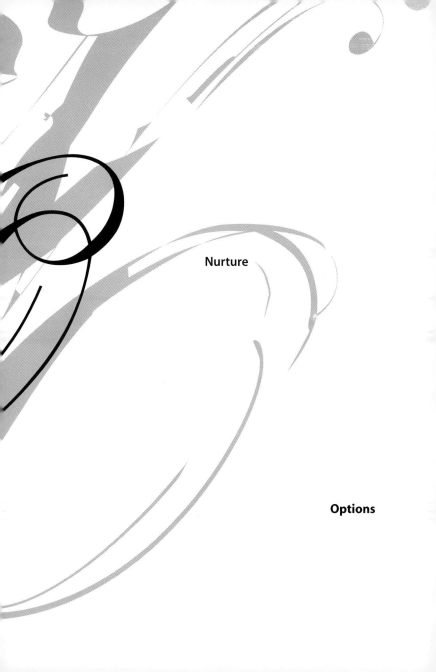

Nurture

Options

Perspective

Perfectionism

Pain

Procrastination

Prejudice

Practice

Purpose

Perspective

We see the world from our perspective and not as it actually is.

Perfectionism

Perfectionism kills our possibilities and so we strive for excellence.

Pain

There is no growth without pain.

Procrastination

Is the thief of our time.

Prejudice

A woman with an unkempt appearance entered a salon and two of the three stylists made themselves scarce thinking that the woman was beneath their standards. The third stylist immediately attended to her needs and when the service was complete, the woman placed a large stack of cash on the counter with the comment, "Let me know when you have gone through this and I will bring you more".

Practice

Practice, practice, practice. We practice discernment. We practice patience. We make progress.

Purpose

Our purpose gives us an excited anticipation of what each day holds for us and promises us new relationships, experiences and adventures

Question

When was the last
time I went to a
museum, the theater,
danced, painted, wrote or
read a poem or told someone I
loved them?

When was the last time I did something for someone and
kept it a secret?

When did I last deliver an overdue apology to someone,
bring flowers to a loved one, took a day trip, called an old
friend, gave thanks?

Or, sat quietly and still, allowed my mind to be inactive and
discovered peace?

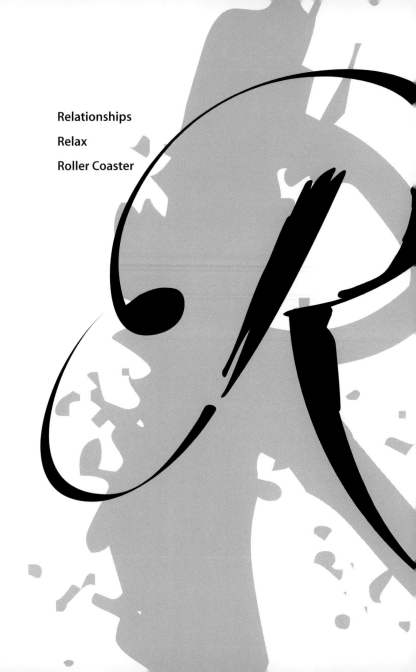

Relationships

Relax

Roller Coaster

Relationships

We maintain relationships with family and friends knowing they are our best support team when times get rough.

Relax

We do

Roller Coaster

Why does this continue to be the most popular ride at amusement parks? We love the peaks and valleys, the thrill and spills, the anticipation and the speed. There is the beginning and an end and the bit in between with the highs and lows...well, that's life!

Self-Talk

We show up, say less and do more, simmer down, seize the moment, set our goals then proceed to work backwards. We realize that some things just are and don't need explaining. Refer to Acceptance.

Self-Talk

We monitor our inner conversation to keep it positive and upbeat. This is how we help our subconscious because it doesn't know the difference between real and unreal. It absorbs whatever we allow inside of us, so we are mindful of the thoughts we entertain.

Teacher

Think

Treat

Trust

Teacher

There is no such thing as failure in our ecosystem, only experience and that is our best teacher. We use everything as a tool for growth.

Think

We think it through: If this, then what? And then what? And then? We can see where our thinking takes us and watch out for our pitfalls. Refer to Self-Talk.

Treat

We treat everyone like a million dollars starting with ourselves.

Trust

We learn to trust our intuition, ourselves, our love, and in trust itself. We are trustworthy to our friends and family.

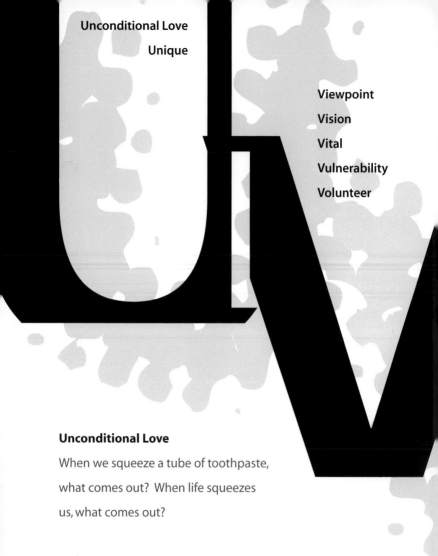

Unconditional Love

Unique

Viewpoint

Vision

Vital

Vulnerability

Volunteer

Unconditional Love

When we squeeze a tube of toothpaste, what comes out? When life squeezes us, what comes out?

Unique

Each of us is unique, one-of-a-kind and complete in every way.

Viewpoint

We find it necessary to change our viewpoint in order to change our point of view.

Vision

If we were to imagine our dream home, how would it look? How would it be decorated, how many rooms, will it have a garden or a pool, what is the color scheme? We can have the same vision of our lives and our chosen occupation.

Vital

Upon visiting their father in the hospital after his last surgery, two friends found the doctors saying there was no more they could do. The father said it has been a great life and if you can, find someone to cut me and I will go under the knife again. He died. Whenever we go for medical treatment, they always check our vitals. How are our vitals?

Vulnerability

We consciously choose to be vulnerable when it is healthy and we share our feelings with those we trust.

Volunteer

There was a man who worked at a construction site and everyday at lunchtime would open his lunch and complain, "Not cheese sandwiches again!" A fellow worker after hearing this scenario for several weeks asked him, "Why don't you get your wife to make you a different sandwich?" The complainer said, "I'm not married." Well then why don't you get your girlfriend to make you a different sandwich? I don't have a girlfriend. Then ask your mother. I live by myself! We unwittingly volunteer for the job of being our own victim.

We

We

Don't panic.

Don't make decisions when upset.

Do dance as if no one is watching.

Do embrace all of life.

Do the do!

We

Don't argue on behalf of our limitations because when we do, we get to own them.

X

Yes

Yesterday

Zest

X

X marks the spot! We are out searching
for gold when we are standing on
buried treasure. We turn the shovel and
dig into ourselves and find the real
precious jewels.

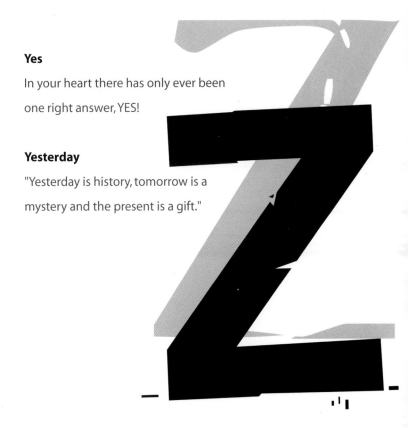

Yes

In your heart there has only ever been
one right answer, YES!

Yesterday

"Yesterday is history, tomorrow is a
mystery and the present is a gift."

Zest

Our Zest for life keeps us moving and creating.